THE SECURE EXECUTIVE™

---

*The Secret of
Becoming One,
Being One,
Staying One*

Steve Kahn

BERKLEY BOOKS, NEW YORK

*This book is dedicated to Andrew Paul Kahn
(a future SE), the product of the best
Secure Executive decision my wife Evelyn
(an SE in her own right) and I have made.*

"The Secure Executive," "The SE," and "SE" are
Trademarks of Steve Kahn.

This Berkley book contains the complete
. text of the original hardcover edition.

THE SECURE EXECUTIVE

A Berkley Book / published by arrangement with
the author

PRINTING HISTORY
G. P. Putnam's Sons edition published 1986
Berkley trade paperback edition / November 1987

ISBN: 0-425-10418-4

A BERKLEY BOOK ® TM 757,375
Berkley Books are published by The Berkley Publishing Group,
200 Madison Avenue, New York, New York 10016.
The name "BERKLEY" and the "B" logo
are trademarks belonging to Berkley Publishing Corporation.

PRINTED IN THE UNITED STATES OF AMERICA

10   9   8   7   6   5   4   3   2   1

Acknowledgments

To Tim W. Ferguson, editorial features editor of *The Wall Street Journal*, who published the two original columns that became the basis of *The Secure Executive*.

To Roger Cooper, whose editorial and marketing vision is the source of the publishing commitment that produced *The Secure Executive* with an uncommonly intense level of TLC.

To Ron Taft, father of Maggie and lawyer/magician, who enabled me to concentrate on the creative aspects while he "took care of business."

To H. I. (Sonny) Bloch, for his friendship and encouragement.

To John S. Tamerin, for his insight and affection.

To "The Thursday Night Group," for its support.

And to my one-of-a-kind wife, Evy, the heart and soul, core and catalyst of whatever SE attributes I possess.

Foreword

The Secure Executive is for and about all of us who are engaged in the process of integrating our lives within the framework of the workplace. I unconditionally believe that each of us has the capacity to become an SE.

If I had to come up with a concise definition of *The SE*, it would simply be: "The secret of winning without losing yourself." With the emphasis on *yourself*.

Being centered, having firmly planted roots, reflecting a character which is consistent and confident: These are the "secrets" of becoming, being and staying an SE.

If they are already up front in your life, then this book will joyfully confirm your status as an SE. If they are still latent, then hopefully you can now begin to move them forward to enable you to balance all of the challenging and sometimes conflicting aspects of your life.

You can do it and, if you are motivated, you will do it, with or without this book. But, judging from the early response, *The SE* may help you to accelerate the process.

One other thought: The use of "he" and "his" throughout denotes all of us, male and female. *The Secure Executive* has no gender. *The SE* is every man and every woman determined to make living and working a qualitative as well as a quantitative experience.

The SE's favorite time of day is now.

———————————————
———————————————

Getting it done is what the SE is all about. Putting it off is not. Now precludes never.

The SE always returns his phone calls the same day.

To many (those afraid of making decisions), a phone call threatens to become a catalyst for decision-making. To an SE, a phone call holds the promise of opportunity. And, even beyond the possibilities of opportunity or discovery, the SE simply considers returning phone calls ASAP a fundamental courtesy.

*The SE keeps his
office door open.*

The SE not only manages by wandering around, he also manages by letting others have the freedom—and the explicit encouragement—to wander in.

The SE never lies.

For three reasons. One, it's totally against his own moral code. Two, he agrees with the adage: "No man has a good enough memory to make a successful liar." Three, if he catches anyone lying, he does not give him a second chance. Ever.

The SE never asks his secretary to buy a birthday present for his spouse.

The SE never blurs the nature and the boundaries of his relationships. Therefore, the converse *doesn't* hold— and the SE would not hesitate to ask his spouse to buy a birthday present for his secretary!

The SE's favorite advertising medium is direct response.

———————————————

Whether it's an 800 number, a coupon in a Sunday newspaper supplement or a catalog targeted by ZIP Code, the SE is not afraid to find out the strength (or weakness) of his product or service as quickly and unambiguously as possible. Obviously, not all products or services lend themselves to direct response, but where DR is appropriate, the SE will go for it every time.

The SE always flies coach on short flights.

The SE's status comes from within, not without. He also passes on the reserved executive parking space. If he's in early, he'll take the best available spot. If he's not, he'll walk the extra aisle. On a long transcontinental or international flight, however, he'll have no hesitation about flying Business Class or even First Class if he can justify the expense by the resulting productivity rather than simply rationalizing the cost.

The SE knows that "no"
reversed says "ON!"

He also knows when to say no.

*The SE tries to do business
only with those he would
invite home for dinner.*

———————————

The SE tries to do business with compatible people. Insofar as possible (and practical), he will avoid building relationships with others whose values are markedly incompatible with his.

The SE believes that quality is as important as quantity.

That applies to quality of earnings as well as to the quality of product or service. The SE doesn't go after inflated sales figures but after maximum bottom-line results achieved by creative, productive management. He would rather net 12 percent on a million dollars than 6 percent on two million. Similarly, the SE will pass on a bid or an opportunity if the specifications can be met only by compromising standards. The SE is a long-distance runner, not someone looking for shortcuts which might lead to dead ends.

The SE won't deliberately lose a golf match, a poker game or Trivial Pursuit to win a client's favor.

The SE plays it straight in the office and won't compromise on any playing field. (And a client whose ego is so fragile and/or insecure as to require "gimmes" is not a client who's going to be comfortable with an SE in the first place.)

The SE believes that an MBA is like a kiss—nothing more than a suggestion of the possibilities.

Case studies, no matter how pragmatically presented, aren't real-life experiences. If the SE were a police chief, he'd make his MBA recruits walk a beat. As an SE, he makes them take the heat.

The SE's desk may be rectangular, but his conference area always has a round table.

You've never heard of a "rectangular table discussion." But "roundtable discussion" has become a part of the business language—and there's more than symbolism involved. A round table is free of edges, and the SE wants conversations free of unnatural barriers as well. Round tables encourage participation and remove distinctions between the participants.

The SE wants his lawyer to tell him why—not why not.

The SE knows that some lawyers consider it their job to kill deals rather than ratify them. Knowing that, the SE is prepared to rebut an attorney's deal-killing instinct—unless he is convinced that it's justifiable homicide.

*The SE wants his accountant
to tell him why not.*

The SE wants to minimize the possibility of subverting careful, prudent long-range planning by unrealistic projections or questionable short-term accounting gamesmanship. He has standing instructions to his numbers crunchers: "Give me the worst-case scenario."

The SE never oversleeps.

The SE also sleeps well, knowing that during the day just ended he did the best he could. Therefore, he can go to bed without regrets or self-doubt. But his inner alarm won't let him sleep away the coming day; his optimistic sense of the dawning possibilities is stronger than any cricket, rooster or clock radio!

The SE always wears his wedding band, even on business trips.

———————————————

The SE does not regard fidelity as currency.

The SE never misses an Open School Night, Little League games or Christmas Eve.

━━━━━━━━━━━━━━━━━━━━

The SE is rooted, and he has no uncertainty about his priorities. His children, in turn, are SCs—Secure Children.

The SE takes his children to the office.

He doesn't do it often or to flaunt his corner office and impressive environment. He does it to integrate his life—and theirs.

The SE does windows.

Which is to say that the SE isn't afraid of taking on some of the more unattractive or unappealing tasks that make up the details of everyday working and living. The SE will never ask anyone to do anything that he wouldn't do himself.

*The SE isn't afraid to learn
computer basics.*

Or whatever else it takes to communicate in our satellite society. And whatever else it takes for him to comprehend every aspect of his business. The SE knows that MIS isn't an abbreviation for Helen Gurley Brown.

The SE's least favorite color is beige.

Beige reflects neutrality, even indecisiveness. The SE is neither neutral nor indecisive.

The SE forgives,
but doesn't forget.

To forgive may be divine, but to forget would be bad management. The SE doesn't hold grudges, doesn't keep black books filled with negative notes, but he does expect subordinates to learn from past mistakes or misjudgments.

The SE believes in research
but makes decisions on
instinct.

The SE won't jump into the pool until he knows how deep it is. Determining the depth is an objective piece of research; deciding to jump in is a subjective piece of timing, desire and opportunity. Similarly, the SE will not make decisions blindly, but will seek as much market information as possible in advance of D-Day. But the ultimate decision—to go or not to go, to do or not to do—will inevitably always be a judgment call. The SE knows that his singular value is his judgment—and his willingness to exercise it.

The SE believes "perks" is a verb, not a pronoun.

The SE doesn't care what others do with their Frequent Flyer goodies, but he begins to worry when they seem to selfishly paraphrase John F. Kennedy: "It's not what I can do for the company, but what the company can do for me!"

*The SE believes in putting up,
not putting down.*

When the father of a college football superstar announced the selection of the agent who would represent his son, he revealed that the winner was the only contender who had not even once put down his competitors. Obviously an SE, he had consistently spoken about what he would do, not what the others couldn't do. The SE is anxious to be put to the test, to be given the opportunity to perform. This self-confidence enables him to sell himself successfully without having to sell out others.

The SE believes that the relationship between believe and achieve is more than simply a rhyme.

━━━━━━━━━━━━━━━━━━━━━━━

The SE knows that you will be unable to achieve unless you believe in yourself and in what you're doing. There's no "but" here: this is an absolute. If you don't believe, you won't achieve. Period.

The SE never holds meetings before eight o'clock.

In this instance, the SE is not being kind to others but to himself. He cherishes his early morning time and uses it to sort out the day's priorities. The SE is not a mythical figure, or even a workaholic, but he is a model of efficacy—and he's learned that meetings which begin any earlier are not in full gear.

The SE never holds meetings after eight o'clock.

The SE does not consider unnecessary stress to be a virtue. Late meetings inevitably create social dislocations, which inevitably lead to unnecessary stress.

The SE isn't afraid to order a chef's salad for lunch.

──────────────────────

Rare steaks and red wine might be considered traditional executive fare, with any substitutions suggesting weakness. The SE, however, defines weakness as giving in to the expected rather than the appropriate.

The SE respects his subordinates' weekends.

The SE respects his subordinates' weekends except when three competitive conglomerates are planning a hostile takeover.

The SE's confident style of management is founded on the ordinary demands of business. When extraordinary events explode, the SE expects total, unconditional commitment from himself—and his people. Suddenly, all the rules dissolve and everyone is expected to participate and perform without regard to any other commitments until the problem is solved. This is the one ultimate test which the SE will not allow anyone to fail.

*The SE isn't afraid to praise
a subordinate, or make coffee
for his secretary.*

This reflects two of the SE's most attractive qualities. [1] He does not surround himself with colleagues who find themselves unrewarded or unappreciated. [2] He doesn't regard his secretary—or anyone, for that matter—as a member of a lower caste. That's why you're more likely to find the SE in the company cafeteria than the executive dining room.

The SE knows that his greatest skill is listening to others.

Long before Management By Wandering Around (MBWA) became fashionable, the SE was listening to as many people, both inside and outside the company, as he could. Hearing is one of our basic senses, but listening is an art. And it is an art the SE has mastered. Hearing tells you that the trees are rustling; listening tells you that a storm is coming and what direction it's coming from!

The SE knows that his second greatest skill is getting others to listen to him.

———————————————

The SE, like Johnny Carson, perspires before speaking in public. And, like a good psychiatrist, he probably prefers talking to others one-on-one. Yet, by practice and performance, the SE has learned how to hold an audience of any size. His basic premise is the same under either circumstance: Respect your audience; give them a sense of the possibilities; and motivate them in a positive environment that removes the fear of failure and encourages expressions of courage.

The SE wears cotton, has a greengrocer, and knocks on wood.

━━━━━━━━━━━━━━━━━━━

The common denominator, of course, is *natural*. South Carolina's cotton, Florida's oranges and Maine's wood are all substances created in nature, not under microscopes or in test tubes. This sense of nature, of being in touch with the basics of life and of living, pervades the SE's sensibilities. He knows—and values—the difference between the real and the synthetic, in products and in people.

The SE never says "Never!"

---

ever is absolute; circumstances are not. Therefore, the SE never says "Never!" But he has been known to say "Not now."

The SE isn't afraid to have comfortable chairs in his office.

———————————

The chairs are simply a representation of corporate turf. The SE, like any player, prefers the home field advantage; but, like all winners, he is not afraid of playing (and winning) on the road. So he's not looking to make his visitors uncomfortable or uneasy, at home or away.

The SE doesn't create false deadlines.

The SE expects real deadlines to be met, but he won't ask others to rush when it's not necessary. And he won't authorize the use of express delivery services unless the material "absolutely, positively" has to be there. Time *is* money—unless there's time to spare, in which case both money and needlessly frayed nerves can be saved.

*The SE isn't afraid to take
a three-week vacation.*

The SE doesn't consider himself indispensable (or else he would consider himself a failure as a manager). Nor does he worry about not being missed, since he is able to distinguish between indispensable and valuable. He has no doubt about his value and no doubt about his right to break away for reasonable periods of R and R. Consequently, he may not call in even once during his vacation. But everyone will know where he is and how to reach him.

*The SE never puts his name
to another's memo.*

If others have contributed data to the report, the SE will not make specific attribution unless acknowledgment enhances the data's impact or validity. But if others have contributed essential concepts, the SE will prominently credit their input. However, this paragraph is philosophically moot—because the SE doesn't believe in memos!

The SE is suspicious of those who wear suspenders with a belt.

The SE has no quarrel with caution where it's appropriate. But he has no patience for those who play it so safe as to virtually immobilize their thoughts and actions.

The SE agrees with Harry S Truman that "The buck stops here."

He also agrees with HST that if you can't stand the heat, you should stay out of the kitchen. In baseball, the most highly regarded players are so-called game players: confident athletes who hope that the ball will be hit to them in a crucial situation. Then there are those players who hope that the ball will be hit anywhere on the field *except* in their direction. The SE is a game player.

The SE likes himself.
The SE likes others.

The SE trusts himself.
The SE trusts others.

━━━━━━━━━━━━━━━━━━

The sense of security which creates and defines the SE can come only from within. It never works if it is a charade or a mask or posturing. Thus, the SE must begin with genuine regard for his own character and values. If he doesn't like himself, he will not be able to like and appreciate his colleagues. If he doesn't trust himself, he will be unable to rely comfortably on others. Understandably, this concrete dimension of unconditional self-confidence can take some time to develop. But it has to be in place, anchored and real, for the SE to sustain his S.

The SE thinks Oreos taste just as good as David's Cookies.

The SE understands and appreciates (and has been known to create) fads. But he doesn't pass on items because they are old-fashioned or "tried-and-true." He knows that they wouldn't have achieved that status if they hadn't managed to survive the challengers who tried to knock them off. The SE, like most of us, is ready to embrace the better mousetrap. But it will have to be not only better, but cost-effective as well!

*The SE doesn't harbor
animals on his weekend
wardrobe.*

The SE doesn't label others, and refuses to be labeled. He also knows who he is—and he knows that he isn't related to Ralph Lauren!

The SE wears penny loafers to the office.

━━━━━━━━━━━━━━━━━━━━━━

They're smartly polished and not run down at the heels, but they are comfortable. And when it comes to a choice between comfort (which enables him to work better) and tradition (which may please the Chairman of the Executive Committee), the SE will always opt for comfort. He's even been known to roll up his sleeves!

The SE always signs in ink.

Pencils and even ballpoint pens can be altered in transit or lost in reproduction. The SE uses a real pen with permanent ink to acknowledge his decisions.

The SE reads his own mail.

Much of it is junk mail and some of it is looking to extract time or money from him, but all of it is addressed to him, not his assistant or his secretary. Only one category of mail offends the SE: Envelopes marked "personal and confidential" that are neither.

The SE doesn't have an
unlisted home telephone.

Unless he's in a business that makes it advisable. No matter what business he's in, all of his people have his number, unpublished or not, with the understanding that the access is to be used appropriately. The SE doesn't appreciate calls at awkward hours, but he never wants to have to ask, "Why didn't you call?"

The SE reads Forbes, Business Week, *and* People.

He also reads *The Wall Street Journal,* his hometown papers and more trade journals than he believes his line of work justifies. He also reads *Sports Illustrated, Family Circle, Variety* and whatever other publications he feels he needs to stay in touch with the world. Which explains why the SE knows his competitors' share of the market as fluently as he knows the value of the pound, Dave Winfield's batting average, the box office receipts of Eddie Murphy's newest movie, and why Campbell's Soup For One (whose ads he saw in a women's magazine) is the likely harbinger of profound cultural and marketing changes.

The SE watches 60 Minutes, This Week with David Brinkley, *and* The Bill Cosby Show.

Different medium, similar premise. However, one personal distinction can be made: While the SE obviously watches television commercials, he will typically respond more passionately to advertisements in print.

*The SE's favorite seven-letter
word is options.*

A more elegant word might be *visions*. No matter what you call it, it is one of the SE's fundamental abilities: to envision all of the possibilities in advance of making a decision. Knowing that he has considered all of the conscious, rational possibilities, the SE has no nagging regrets after the decision has been made. To some degree, this is an innate gift; but to an even greater extent, perceiving all possible options is a learned discipline requiring patience, intelligence and imagination. SE 101!

The SE isn't afraid to laugh.

Many studies asking people what quality they appreciate most in others report that the number one virtue is a good sense of humor. Yet, how many people do we know who are that cheerfully and consistently virtuous? The SE is. He doesn't go around telling jokes, but he does evoke the humorous side of events, thereby easing tensions. It is an important and valuable quality in an often difficult world. The *Reader's Digest* is right: Laughter *is* the best medicine! And the SE knows it, too.

The SE isn't afraid to cry.

Whereas, regarding humor, the SE literally engages in laughter, in this example crying represents the SE's ability to empathize with his colleagues. The SE's sensitivity to the people he works with and the environment he lives in is well established. But the point is that it has to be a spontaneous sensitivity, reactive and responsive and real. The SE has the ability—and the humanity—to transmit it.

*The SE is in no hurry
to grow up.*

The objective is to retain the innocence and open-mindedness and reflexive playfulness of childhood. Sure, the SE (like most of us over twenty-one) has to act and dress "grown-up." But the SE also works at retaining (and recalling) those childhood values and memories which will help him gain useful insights during those moments when adult conditioning, by getting in the way of free association, may preclude coming up with an untraditional solution to an unconventional problem. Also, not (entirely) growing up is simply a lot more fun!

The SE does his homework.

In a very practical sense, perhaps this is the one line all spouses and lovers should needlepoint for their SEs! It is a fundamental truth in the life of an SE. He does his homework, day after day after day, night after night after night. He does not engage in a casual encounter or a heavy negotiation without having done his homework. He may (and probably will) walk into a meeting without so much as a legal pad in his hand, but his briefcase was bulging on the way in to the office. The SE knows what *everyone* else present is supposed to know, and therefore, the SE is always prepared. SEs aren't omniscient; they simply work a little smarter than the rest of the world!

The SE considers Leo Buscaglia, not Machiavelli, required reading.

The SE knows that unconditional love and indiscriminate hugs won't solve the problems of the world. But he does know that if others are spending their days hatching self-serving schemes, they will undermine his objectives with the certainty of a time bomb. Therefore, he'll take a corporate hugging (Buscaglia) over a corporate mugging (Machiavelli) every time.

The SE knows that
knowledge isn't power.

122

It's simply potential. It's what you do with that information that matters. The SE considers knowledge to be the requisite for taking action; knowledge is the precursor, not the product, of power. Therefore, the SE won't tolerate action unsupported by research and sound reasoning.

The SE never asks more of others than he asks of himself.

Generals who lead armies from behind the lines are soldiers who lose battles. The executive who wants that report on his desk by nine the next morning and issues that directive while leaving the office at the stroke of five is an executive at the threshold of a staff rebellion. The SE is an equal opportunity leader. If he asks you to bust your butt, he will ask no less of himself.

The SE wants to win (and usually does)—but he also cares about how he plays the game.

Amen.